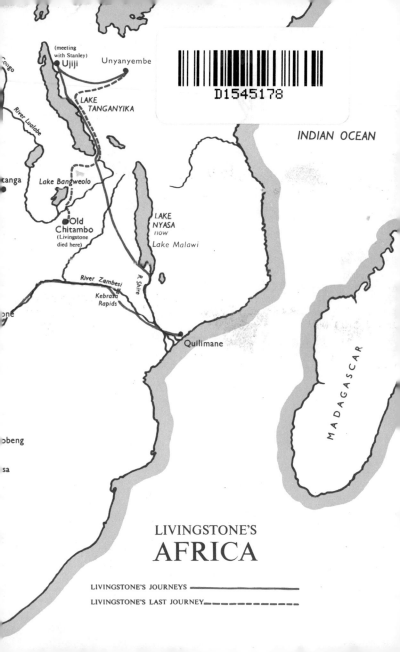

(meeting with Stanley)
Ujiji Unyanyembe

LAKE TANGANYIKA

River Lualaba

:anga

Lake Bangweolo

Old Chitambo
(Livingstone died here)

LAKE NYASA
now
Lake Malawi

River Zambesi
Kebrasa Rapids

R. Shire

INDIAN OCEAN

one

Quilimane

MADAGASCAR

obeng

sa

LIVINGSTONE'S
AFRICA

LIVINGSTONE'S JOURNEYS ————

LIVINGSTONE'S LAST JOURNEY ———————

Series 561

David Livingstone was one of the great men who lived during the reign of Queen Victoria. He was the first white man to explore the wildest parts of central Africa, and his adventures would fill many books.

This is something of his story.

David Livingstone

by L. DU GARDE PEACH, MA PhD DLitt

with illustrations
by JOHN KENNEY

Ladybird Books Loughborough

DAVID LIVINGSTONE

David Livingstone, one of the greatest of missionary explorers, was born in Scotland at a small village called Blantyre, in the year 1813.

When Livingstone afterwards wrote the story of his life, he said: " At the age of ten I went to the factory as a ' piecer.' With part of my first week's wages I purchased ' Rudiments of Latin ' and studied the language for many years with unabated ardour at an evening school, which met between the hours of eight and ten. I continued my labours when I got home till midnight or even later, if my mother did not interfere by snatching the books out of my hands. I had to be back at the factory by six in the morning, and my work lasted, with intervals for breakfast and dinner, till eight o'clock at night."

It was a hard life for a boy, but young David Livingstone was determined to learn all he could. This desire for knowledge remained with him to the end. The result was that he not only learnt more about Africa than any white man had ever known before, but he passed his hard-won knowledge on to the world.

David Livingstone's father and mother were devout Christians, and by the time he was twenty years old David had decided to devote his life to preaching the Gospel of Christ in foreign lands. He made up his mind to go to China as a missionary.

It was at this early period of his life that David Livingstone came to the conclusion that whilst converting the Chinese people to Christianity, he could also help them in other ways by becoming a doctor as well as a missionary.

Although he was still employed in the mill, he started to learn medicine by propping his books up on the spinning machine and, as he says, " catching sentence after sentence " as he worked.

Soon he was earning enough in the summer to enable him to attend medical classes in Glasgow during the winter, and in 1840, when he was twenty-seven years old, he qualified as a doctor.

David Livingstone felt that he was now ready to begin his life's work.

The year 1840 saw the outbreak of war between England and China, and this meant that Livingstone could not become a missionary in that country. Instead, he joined the London Missionary Society.

In London, the young Scot made many new friends. Amongst these was Dr. Moffat, a well-known missionary from Africa, who was lecturing about his work in what was called the Dark Continent. Dr. Moffat was a fine and good man, and Livingstone felt that it would be a wonderful thing to follow his example and preach to the people of Africa.

At a London meeting he asked Dr. Moffat if there was work for him in Africa. " Yes," said Dr. Moffat, " if you are willing to push on to the vast unoccupied district to the north, where on a clear morning I have seen the smoke of a thousand native villages, where no missionary has ever been."

Dr. Moffat's advice decided the whole course of Livingstone's career.

Livingstone wanted nothing better than such an opportunity to carry the Word of God into new, unexplored country. In December, 1840, he set sail for Africa.

The voyage to the Cape of Good Hope took three months. There were, of course, no fast steamships, and sailing ships were often becalmed for days together when there was no wind to fill the sails. It was very easy for people to become bored on voyages of this sort.

Livingstone was never bored. He was always eager to learn anything that would be useful to him, and on the long voyage to Africa he persuaded the Captain of the ship to teach him how to use a quadrant. This was an instrument employed by sailors to find their exact position at sea.

Because of this knowledge, when Livingstone was later exploring distant parts of Africa, he was able to make accurate maps of country which had never before been visited by a white man.

When Livingstone arrived in Africa he went first to the most northerly mission station in the country. This was at a place called Kuruman, seven hundred miles north of Cape Town, and the missionary in charge was his friend Dr. Moffat.

To the north of Kuruman the country was completely unknown to white settlers. It was largely desert and was inhabited by savage tribes like the Matabele, who from time to time raided the white settlements to the south of them, killing men, women and children.

It was on a journey into this dangerous and difficult country that Livingstone set out before he had been a year in Africa. He travelled seven hundred miles round the edge of the desert, partly in an ox-wagon and partly on foot.

Two years later, in 1842, he started a mission station at Mabotsa, two hundred miles north of Kuruman, far from all other white men, surrounded by savage tribes.

After living alone at Mabotsa for two years, Livingstone married Dr. Moffat's daughter, Mary, and Livingstone tells how they spent their time learning the native languages, preaching the Gospel, healing the sick, and getting to know all they could about the country. It was a happy marriage, for although there was a serious side to his nature, Livingstone had a keen sense of humour, and when opportunity offered, was always ready for what he called " merriment and play."

At the same time, he never stopped learning. Believing that all knowledge is useful he started to study geology. This means knowing all about the rocks and soil which make up the earth. It was to be very useful to Livingstone in the years ahead.

Very soon Livingstone and his wife felt that they ought to go further north into the country of tribes who had not yet heard the word of God. In 1847 they built a new mission station with their own hands, eighty miles north of Mabotsa, at a place called Kolobeng.

Here they lived happy, busy lives for the next five years.

Livingstone never forgot that his chief reason for being in Africa was to convert the natives. Christianity was so different from the way in which they lived and thought, that they found it very difficult to understand.

One of the chiefs of the Bechuana tribe, whose name was Sechele, was converted by Livingstone, and decided that it would be a good thing if the whole tribe became Christians. But his method of converting people was different from Livingstone's.

" My people will never believe by your just talking to them," he said. " I can only make them do things by beating them. If you like, I will call my head men with their whips, and we will soon make all the people in the tribe Christians together."

This was not at all what Livingstone intended, and he persuaded the chief to let him preach to the people instead. Soon Sechele was surprised to find that Livingstone was able to persuade the natives to become Christians without the aid of whips. The Gospel of Peace was not to be taught by violence.

A great deal of Livingstone's time was taken up by healing the sick. As soon as it became known that there was a white man who could bring relief to their sufferings, natives would walk hundreds of miles to consult him.

Wherever he was, Livingstone would set up a makeshift surgery, often just a table under a sheet stretched between two trees. Here, in the shade, he used to treat the savage warriors who stood silently waiting for their turn.

They were very good patients. Even when he had to operate on them with his sharp surgical knives, they never winced. They would sit and talk as though they felt nothing.

" Men like us never cry," they would say. " It is only children that cry."

Because Livingstone cared for them and cured them, the most savage natives soon learnt to love and trust him.

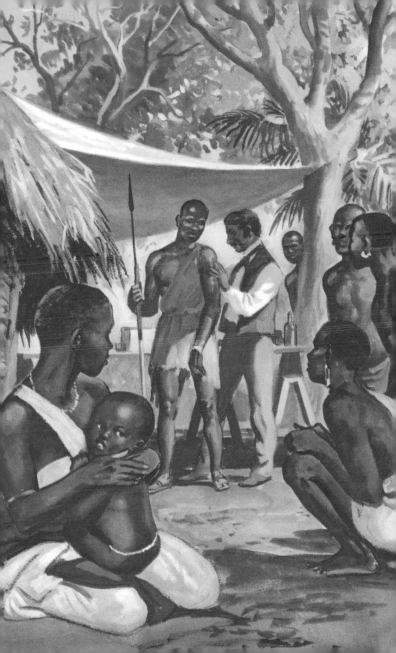

As well as preaching to the natives and curing them when they were ill, Livingstone spent much of his time exploring wild and uncharted parts of Africa. He already knew how to find his exact position by using the quadrant; now he learnt how to make maps of the country through which he was travelling.

Two years after building his house at Kolobeng, Livingstone made his first great journey northwards, across the Kalahari desert, to Lake Ngami. He and two hunters, who were with him, were the first white men ever to see this lake in the middle of the great waste of the African desert.

This was a journey of hundreds of miles through most difficult and almost waterless country, but nothing daunted Livingstone. The following year he again made the journey, this time accompanied by his wife and three small children, all dressed much as they would have been in England. This must have seemed like one long picnic to the children, with a father and mother who were always ready to play with them and have fun.

Livingstone now decided to explore the country northwards from Lake Ngami. He felt that somewhere, not very far away, he would find country which could be settled by white farmers.

So he went to Cape Town for supplies, and after nine months of travelling through alternate droughts and floods, Livingstone, together with a coloured trader named Fleming, reached Linyanti, two hundred miles north-east of Lake Ngami. Here Fleming left him, but Livingstone stayed on for a short while, preaching, teaching, healing the sick, and preparing for the journey he hoped to make across Africa to the west coast.

Livingstone describes the Makololo natives, amongst whom he was now living, as the finest in Africa. Their chief, Sekeletu, a young man of eighteen, became his very good friend.

But it was here that Livingstone first became ill with malaria, and for the rest of his life he was seldom free from it.

After six months in Linyanti, Livingstone set off north-westwards. His object was to find out whether there was a possible route from Linyanti to the Atlantic coast.

Livingstone took very little equipment with him on his travels. A small gipsy tent to sleep in, a sheepskin mantle as a blanket, and a horse rug as a bed. But he never forgot to take quinine, the best medicine for warding off malarial fever.

It was a very long way to the sea, about three thousand miles by the way Livingstone went, through country never before travelled by a white man.

The party consisted of Livingstone himself and twenty-seven natives from various tribes. They travelled by canoe where it was possible, with some of the men driving the oxen along the bank; and at night they camped, in Livingstone's own words, in " perfect peace."

Crocodiles and hippopotomi infested the rivers, and great care was necessary to avoid overturning the canoes.

Livingstone reached the coast in just over six months, at a place called Loanda, a town belonging to the Portuguese.

All the way across Africa Livingstone had marked his route on the map which he was making. Whatever dangers or hardships he met by the way, there were two things which Livingstone never failed to do each evening—to say his prayers, and to find out his exact position by means of his quadrant.

On one of his journeys, when Livingstone was travelling with another white man, he stopped and picked up some pebbles. He looked at them and threw them away.

Many days later the white man remembered this and asked Livingstone what they were. " They were diamonds," said Livingstone, who had recognised them because he had studied geology. " Can you find the place again ? " asked the man. " Yes," said Livingstone, " but you can't."

Livingstone knew that if he told anyone where the diamonds were, men would come swarming there from all over the world, and the simple way of life, which the natives enjoyed, would be destroyed for ever.

Livingstone returned to Linyanti by the same route, meaning to begin another journey, this time to the east coast.

He set off with his faithful porters, and a very short journey down the Zambesi river brought him to one of the greatest wonders of the world.

The natives called this *MOSI-OA-TUN-YA*, which means "the smoke which sounds." By this name they described the spray, high in the air, and the thunder of the falling water from a waterfall a mile wide and twice as high as Niagara.

Livingstone christened the great waterfall "The Victoria Falls," after the then reigning Queen, and they are still marked on the map by this name.

Before Livingstone discovered the Victoria Falls, no white man had ever seen them. To-day a railway runs close by, and many tourists visit them every year. The town that has been built on the bank of the river is called Livingstone, in honour of the great missionary and explorer.

After many adventures Livingstone reached Quilimane, a little seaport belonging to the Portuguese, where the Zambesi river runs into the Indian Ocean.

Here a brig of the British Navy took him aboard. After a month in Mauritius, to recover from malaria (which had seriously weakened him), Livingstone returned to England in a steamship. It was sixteen years since he had left his native country.

During that time Livingstone had travelled further into darkest Africa than any other white man, and had crossed the great Continent from one side to the other.

In England Livingstone was greeted as a hero. He received a gold medal from the Royal Geographical Society, and the City of London honoured him by making him a Freeman of the City.

Everywhere he went crowds gathered to cheer him, and on one occasion he had to jump into a cab in Regent Street to escape from them.

Livingstone had proved that there was new and perhaps profitable country to be discovered on the Zambesi river. Soon the newspapers and the people were saying that the Government ought to help him to make more journeys of exploration.

Before Livingstone had been very long in England he was sent for by the Foreign Secretary, Lord Clarendon.

This was a great thing for Livingstone. On his earlier journeys he was not able to buy all that he really required, and as a result he had suffered many hardships. This was now all changed.

" Tell me what you want," said Lord Clarendon, and Livingstone suggested that seven men, each trained to do some particular part of the work, should be paid to go with him.

The result was that the Government granted him £5,000. At the same time he was appointed British Consul at Quilimane at a salary of £500 a year.

With money at his disposal Livingstone was able to fit out a better expedition. He had now left the London Missionary Society, and although he still meant to preach to the natives wherever he went, he was free to give more of his time to exploring the unknown parts of Africa.

One thing which Livingstone needed to follow the course of the Zambesi river was a small steamboat. Previously he had only canoes paddled by the natives, and he hoped that the steamboat would make things very much easier.

Unfortunately the steamboat was very old, because Livingstone had not enough money to buy a new one. It leaked badly and the engines were always breaking down. In spite of this, and the fact that the officer commanding the steamboat had left the expedition, Livingstone started off up the Zambesi river from Quilimane.

The Zambesi divides when it reaches the sea into a number of different streams called a delta. Unfortunately Livingstone mistook the mouth of another river for the Zambesi, and he had to turn back and start all over again.

The second start was more successful. Livingstone was able to steam up the river for three hundred miles, until he came to a place called the Kebrasa rapids.

Here the river was full of great rocks and the swirling waters were foaming over them between the high banks. The steamboat could go no further.

So again Livingstone turned back and was soon steaming up another unexplored river, the Shire. He was no more fortunate than he had been on the Zambesi. Again rocks and rapids made it impossible for the steamboat to go on.

But Livingstone had heard from the natives of a great lake to the northward, and he was determined to find it.

Setting off on foot, Livingstone travelled another two hundred miles north until he came to the southern end of a lake which stretched out of sight. This was Lake Nyasa, one of the three greatest lakes in Africa.

Livingstone was the first white man ever to set eyes on it.

The expedition which Livingstone had planned so carefully met with many misfortunes. All the men who came out with him from England had left, with the exception of one, afterwards famous as Sir John Kirk of Zanzibar.

In another way, however, this expedition had more important results than almost any of Livingstone's earlier journeys.

What was known as "the slave trade" was being carried on all over this part of Africa. Men, women and children were captured by fierce savages, and then sold as slaves. Livingstone determined to do what he could to stop this terrible state of things.

One day, on the Zambesi river, he and his men came across some armed men with a convoy of slaves, all of whom were chained together.

When Livingstone attacked the guards they ran away, and he was able to free eighty-four slaves. This meant that ever afterwards the men who were making a lot of money by capturing and selling slaves, were Livingstone's bitter enemies.

The savage slave raiders were not long in trying to revenge themselves on Livingstone for having freed the slaves. One day, when he was travelling with a party of missionaries who had come out from England, they were suddenly attacked by the Ajawas.

Livingstone tells in his journal how a large body of savages surrounded his little party and refused to listen when he tried to tell them that he wanted to talk to them, not to fight with them.

" Suddenly," he says, " they closed upon us in bloodthirsty fury. Some came within fifty yards, dancing hideously. They began to shoot their poisoned arrows, and wounded one of our men through the arm. Four were armed with muskets, and we were obliged, in self defence, to return their fire and drive them off. When they saw the range of our rifles they ran away, but some shouted that they would follow us and kill us where we slept."

Livingstone wrote letters to England telling people all about the terrible slave trade. His stories of how the slave traders used to kill the slaves who became too tired to walk, made the Government of England and of many other European countries, determined to put a stop to slave raiding in Africa.

Livingstone now decided to explore Lake Nyasa. He had no idea how large it was, and he would have been very surprised to learn that it was more than three hundred miles from one end to the other.

But he realised that he would need some sort of a boat, and the steamship which he had on the Zambesi was now a wreck. Livingstone decided that a sailing boat was what he needed, but the difficulty was how to get it up to Lake Nyasa.

It could not come up the river and get past the rapids, any more than could the steamboat. There was only one thing to do. Livingstone recruited hundreds of natives and the sailing boat was carried overland, all the hundreds of miles to Lake Nyasa.

The sailing boat was not a success, and Livingstone was again obliged to travel by foot. Notes from his diary show the sort of adventures, very strange to us, which were to him everyday events.

" 13th November 1866. A lion came last night and gave a growl or two on finding that he could not get at our meat. Our people kept up shouting for hours afterwards in order to scare him away.

" 12th January 1867. Sitting down this morning near a tree, my head was just a yard off from a good-sized cobra coiled up at its root, but it was benumbed with cold.

" 20th January 1867. The two Waiyau, who joined us in Kande's village, now deserted. Heavy rain obliterated every vestige of their footsteps. To make the loss more serious, they took what we could least spare—the medicine box, which they would only throw away as soon as they came to examine their booty."

Livingstone now had no quinine with which to guard against the deadly malarial fever.

Because of the loss of the quinine Livingstone became very ill. Stricken by fever, and with very little food, he struggled on until he was forced to return to a place called Ujiji on the east shore of Lake Tanganyika.

All his native bearers had deserted, except three, two of whom, Susi and Chumah, were to remain with him to the end.

No one in England had had any news of Livingstone for four-and-a-half years. Many people thought that he must have been killed by the savages and would never be heard of again.

In order to find out what had happened to him, a young man called Stanley was sent to Africa by an American newspaper. After months of travel, Stanley found Livingstone at Ujiji. This is how he described the meeting:

" I took off my hat and said, ' Dr. Livingstone, I presume ? ' 'Yes,' he said, with a kind smile, lifting his cap slightly, and we shook hands."

It was one of the most famous meetings in history.

Stanley remained with Livingstone for four months. The medical supplies which he had brought from England seemed quickly to restore Livingstone's health and strength.

Together they set out to explore the shores of Lake Tanganyika, travelling by boat. Livingstone hoped to find a river running out of the lake to the north. If they found one, it might prove to be the source of the River Nile.

They were not successful. There is no outlet from Lake Tanganyika to the north. Stanley returned to England, leaving Livingstone at a place called Unyanyembe, where some much needed stores were awaiting him.

Livingstone was now about sixty years old and Stanley describes him as looking ten years younger than his age, still alert and vigorous, and with sight "as keen as a hawk."

As soon as he had collected his supplies Livingstone started off on his last journey with a party of fifty-six porters.

This time Livingstone travelled round the southern end of Lake Tanganyika to Lake Bangweolo. From here he hoped to go westward into Katanga, and then down the river Lomane to the Lualabe, and so back to Ujiji. From Ujiji he proposed to return to England.

But in spite of his appearance, Livingstone was a sick man. He struggled on to Old Chitambo near Lake Bangweolo, and there, on May 1st 1873, he died.

His two faithful native servants, Susi and Chumah, carried his body fifteen hundred miles to the coast. It was brought back to England and David Livingstone, one of the greatest men of the nineteenth century, was buried in Westminster Abbey.

Livingstone had travelled 29,000 miles in Africa and added 1,000,000 square miles to the map. He had discovered six lakes and many rivers and mountains, including the biggest waterfall in the world.

But more important than all, it was due to Livingstone's work and writings that the movement was set on foot which abolished the slave trade in Africa.

Loanda

ATLANTIC OCEAN

Lin

Swamp

Lake Ngami

Kalahari Desert

Kuruman

Orange River

Cape Town